MATHEMATICAL ADVENTURES!

BY
IOANNA GEORGIOU

ILLUSTRATED BY
ASUKA YOUNG

Publisher's Note

Mathematical Adventures is a beautiful, lively journey through history that puts the mathematics we do at school in context. Readers – and their parents and teachers – will see the origins of the techniques and tasks that they do as part of the curriculum. What often is presented out of context, suddenly will have context. As Marcus Garvey put it (albeit about something broader):

"…people without knowledge of …past history, origin and culture [are] like a tree without roots."

Mathematics, like everything else, needs rooting in everyday life, in the excitement of discoveries past, in cultural shifts and past achievements. Taught without that context, there is a danger of "why-do-we-study-this-itis" turning students off.

Readers of this wonderful book will never be in such danger. Even better, in the later chapters the book opens reader's minds to the wider wonderful world of mathematics.

If readers want to learn more, after reading *Mathematical Adventures* – see Ioanna Georgiou's page on the Tarquin site www.tarquingroup.com/MathematicalAdventures. For more on this, and relevant Tarquin titles, see the back of this book.

Mathematical Adventures
© 2019 Ioanna Georgiou
Illustrations by Asuka Young
Book ISBN 978-1-90755-020-1
EBook ISBN 978-1-911093-60-2

Tarquin
Suite 74, 17 Holywell Hill
St Albans
AL1 1DT, UK
www.tarquingroup.com

IOANNA GEORGIOU (AUTHOR)

Ioanna (transliterated to Yo-Anna) has been teaching mathematics ever since she finished her mathematics degree - and maybe a bit before then! The eternal truth found in mathematics fascinates her, and she has been developing her work around teaching and learning mathematics more widely, including developing resources and being an examiner. After her first degree, she went on to complete a Masters in Mathematics Education. She is a Fellow of the Institute of Mathematics and its Applications and a Chartered Mathematics Teacher.

She subsequently conducted research in Teaching Mathematics through History and Culture and earned an MPhil in Education. Her special interest around the use of history and cultural practices in the mathematics teaching continued and she has been delivering masterclasses and workshops on stories from mathematics for the Royal Institution of Great Britain and also independently. This is her attempt to put some of the stories in a book and hopefully get lots of people excited about how mathematics has been changing over the years.

ASUKA YOUNG (ILLUSTRATOR)

Asuka is a self-taught freelance illustrator and Graphic Designer, with a passion for cartoons and all things creative. Asuka has voluntarily taken an active part in the design of marketing materials for some exciting events. And now she is thrilled to be a part of the production for this fantastic educational book, in the hopes to help young people get a glimpse of just where their everyday mathematics content they learn in school actually came from!

Why This Book?

School mathematics sometimes excite and sometimes scare, and sadly, sometimes bore. There is certainly a lack of explanation as to how did all the ideas taught in school come to exist. Further, since everyone contends that mathematics is absolutely essential we seem to be unable to use our algebraic skills in an everyday scenario? In fact, primary school arithmetic seems to get us through most situations. So why all the rest? How did it come up and why?

This book aspires to give a glimpse into how things started and evolved, and how mathematics can help us from simple measurements to navigating ourselves using mathematically simplified tube/subway maps. The stories come up roughly in a chronological order and the accompanying activities (some easier and some more challenging ones) aim to get you engaged with what was happening at a given time.
There are answers and explanations about all tasks in the end of the book.

Acknowledgements

Special thanks to
Azarel Jacobs, Tony Mann and Laura Vroomen
for reading drafts and providing valuable feedback.

CONTENTS...

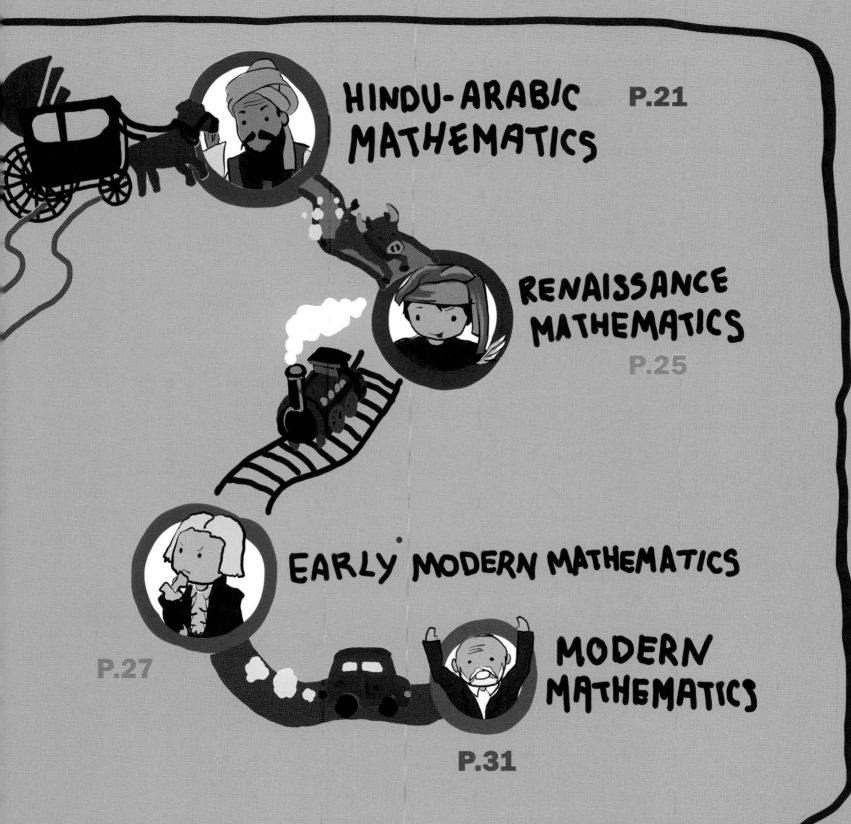

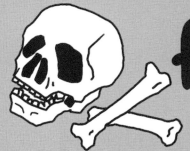

ANCIENT MATHEMATICS

NUMBERING SYSTEMS

What might have been the very first motivation behind some of our earliest mathematical concepts? Counting how much food is available, perhaps? And how best and most efficiently it might be consumed and how much can be used in a given period. Counting how many days before spring arrives and the soil becomes favourable for planting, and then how many days until harvest?

Counting seems to be an obvious requirement for functioning at even the most rudimentary level. Measuring time seems particularly important and must have been tackled early on so that people could track the changing seasons, making best use of the rainy and sunny times to maximise productivity and enhance comfort.

THE LEBOMBO BONE

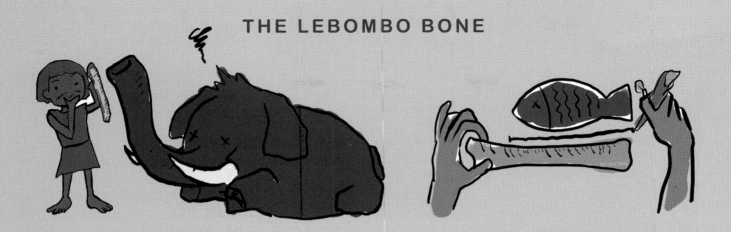

The Lebombo bone is the oldest mathematical artefact we know of. It is around 37,000 years old and it was found in Swaziland. It comes with 29 notches. If you try to think of what it reminds you of, you will probably come up with a ruler. It is perhaps an ancient measuring device – it looks quite rough to our eyes but remember that the need for precision has been relentlessly and inexorably increasing ever since these marks were originally cut. Perhaps it might have been used to count the days in a lunar cycle (from a full moon to the next) which happens to be but half a day more than the 29 represented here.

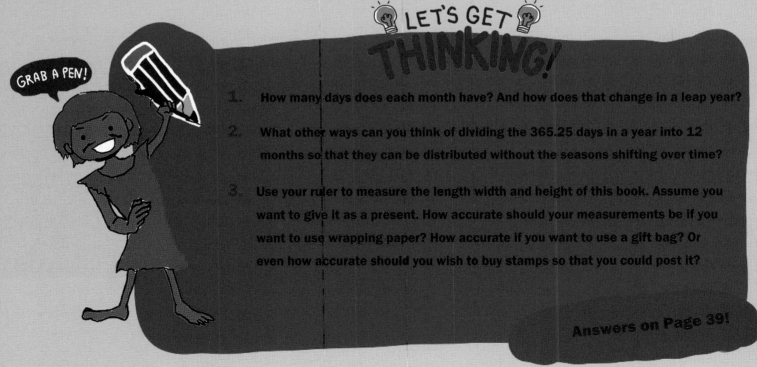

GRAB A PEN!

LET'S GET THINKING!

1. How many days does each month have? And how does that change in a leap year?

2. What other ways can you think of dividing the 365.25 days in a year into 12 months so that they can be distributed without the seasons shifting over time?

3. Use your ruler to measure the length width and height of this book. Assume you want to give it as a present. How accurate should your measurements be if you want to use wrapping paper? How accurate if you want to use a gift bag? Or even how accurate should you wish to buy stamps so that you could post it?

Answers on Page 39!

THE ISHANGO BONE

The Ishango bone is not quite as old as the Lebombo bone; this one is 22,000 years old. Adding up all the notches on this bone we find that there are 168, which is neatly divisible by six; 168 divided by 6 gives us 28. One plausible explanation is that someone was keeping track of the lunar cycles and created a six "month" calendar. But a careful observation of row b reveals a selection of prime numbers. What are prime numbers? And how is it possible that people of those times could have known about them?

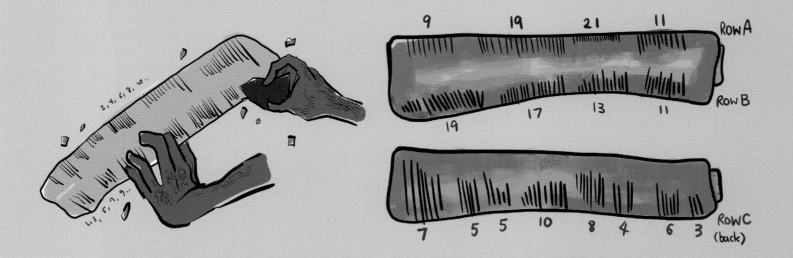

Imagine this scenario: you have just collected seven bananas and brought them back home. There's one for your sister, one for your brother, one for mum, one for dad and one for you, so that's five bananas that are needed to feed everyone at home. You will end up with two left over! You have noticed that whenever you brought home seven of anything, seven mangoes, seven oranges, there are always left overs, even when dad or mum are out or when an auntie visits. It only works that there are no left overs when there is exactly seven of you at home. That does not happen when you come home with six, eight or nine; you can share those ones more easily, sometimes between two, three or four people.

...This inability to share out a quantity of something equally amongst (for example) a group of people is what makes that number a prime number. Nowadays we say that the number is only divisible by itself, and by one. Back then they could have said that the bananas (or oranges or mangoes) can only be shared amongst the same number of people, or even better, kept all for myself!

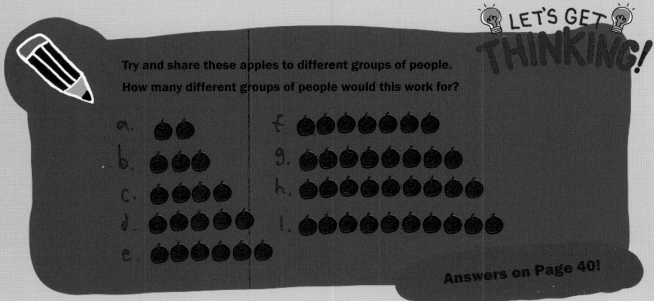

LET'S GET THINKING!

Try and share these apples to different groups of people.
How many different groups of people would this work for?

a. 🍎🍎
b. 🍎🍎🍎
c. 🍎🍎🍎🍎
d. 🍎🍎🍎🍎🍎
e. 🍎🍎🍎🍎🍎🍎
f. 🍎🍎🍎🍎🍎🍎🍎
g. 🍎🍎🍎🍎🍎🍎🍎🍎
h. 🍎🍎🍎🍎🍎🍎🍎🍎🍎🍎
i. 🍎🍎🍎🍎🍎🍎🍎🍎🍎🍎🍎

Answers on Page 40!

EGYPTIANS & THEIR CONTEMPORARIES

NUMBERING SYSTEMS

Once counting had been established, it was natural to want to do calculations. Add, subtract, multiply and divide. There was a need to have ways of representing these calculations efficiently and consistently, so a formal numbering system became increasingly pressing. There have been many numbering systems introduced by various ancient peoples.

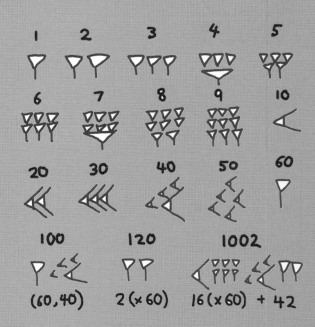

THE BABYLONIAN NUMBERING SYSTEM

The Babylonian system is sexagesimal; this peculiar word means the system has base sixty. This system was quite influential and it is still in use today. We have sixty seconds in a minute and sixty minutes in an hour.

That's why it is sometimes challenging to calculate with time, rather than say, with money. Money is in decimal system, so £1.50 means one pound and fifty pence, whilst 1.5 hours means one hour and thirty minutes. So we need to actually change the digit 5 to a 3 in order to move between the two systems.

Sixty is a number that is particularly easy to use as it is divisible by many other numbers. We call these its factors.

The Factors of Sixty are:

_____

Answers on Page 40!

Now let's make another connection between the Babylonian numbering system and our modern units of measurement. We can find sixty, six times within a full rotation. We know that a full rotation has 360 degrees. This is a number that is easy to manipulate because of the high number of factors it has. This number is a 'Wrong rounding of the number of days in a year'. The duration of a year, 365.25 days, when rounded to the nearest 10 is 370. 370 contains 37 which is prime, hence the amount of factors is only 8 (which?), in contrast to the 24 factors that 360 boasts (which?).

THE MAYAN NUMBERING SYSTEM

The Mayans used a vigesimal system; this means it has base 20. But it also had 5 as a kind of sub-base, in the sense that there is a special symbol for 5 used repeatedly.

The Mayan civilisation came to an end by the 9th century AD and so there was not much opportunity for them to influence other mathematical systems. Their symbol for zero as a place holder was quite unique in its time. There were no zeros in other systems until much later!

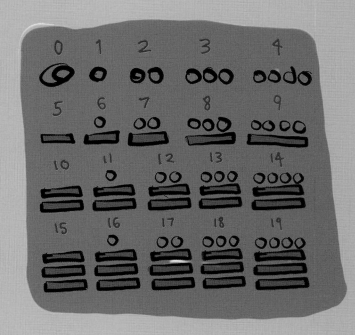

Let's now consider our current numbering system.

THE DECIMAL SYSTEM

As the word suggests, our system has base ten. So what are the common factors in all systems we have seen so far? Indeed, five and ten. Consider what you have been mostly using to help you count and do sums as you were growing up: your fingers! So our whole modern numbering system developed because of how many fingers we have.

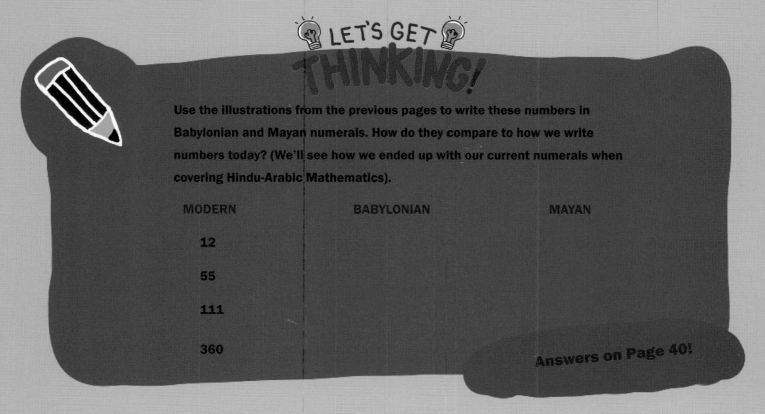

LET'S GET THINKING!

Use the illustrations from the previous pages to write these numbers in Babylonian and Mayan numerals. How do they compare to how we write numbers today? (We'll see how we ended up with our current numerals when covering Hindu-Arabic Mathematics).

MODERN	BABYLONIAN	MAYAN
12		
55		
111		
360		

Answers on Page 40!

THE PYRAMIDS

What is the first thing that comes to mind when we think of Egypt? Probably the pyramids! Majestic structures indeed, and in fact the Great Pyramid of Giza is a sole remaining survivor of the seven wonders of the ancient world. The design skills and knowledge that must have gone into building something that has lasted intact for over 3,500 years must have been quite advanced, and the calculations highly accurate. In Ancient Egypt mathematics was already significantly developed when these pyramids were being conceived and built, with sophisticated taxes, land distribution, produce yield management, trading, and so on.

RHIND MATHEMATICAL PAPYRUS

The Rhind Mathematical Papyrus dates back to 1650 BC and it contains several numerical and geometrical problems. The problems are in line with the practicalities of everyday life. But here is an unexpected problem:

Problem 79: There are seven houses; in each house there are seven cats; each cat kills seven mice; each mouse has eaten seven grains of barley; each grain would have produced seven *hekat**. What is the sum of all the enumerated things?

Answers on Page 40!

***hekat** was a measurement unit for volume.

Before we attempt to solve this, let's take a minute to consider its utility: would solving this poser facilitate any day-to-day challenges likely encountered? Probably not. Then why was this problem recorded? Consider solving today's puzzle books, sudokus, riddles and so on. No practical use there, just curiosity perhaps and amusement. Indeed, here is one of the very first examples of mathematics done for the sake of entertainment alone!

If you were waiting for the time when fractions would appear, this is it! In ancient Egypt, fractions had a numerator of one, what we would now call unit fractions: $\dfrac{1}{any\ number}$

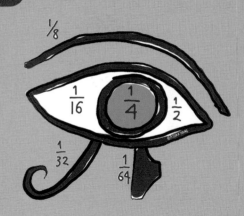

Story of the Eye of Horus

1. There was once a family of Deities: Osiris and his wife Isis, then Seth, Osiris's brother.

OSIRIS

ISIS

SETH

2. Jealous of Osiris's success, Seth assassinates Osiris during a family feast.

3. Isis and Osiris had their son, Horus. Isis ran away to safety with Horus to escape Seth.

5. However during battle Seth gets hold of Horus's eye!

4. Horus grows up into a strong man, and sets out for revenge against Seth.

6. After, the Goddess Hathos came and restored Horus's missing eye.

7. Horus sets out for another revenge and becomes victorious over Seth! The revenge is taken.

8. One day, the Moon God Thoth finds the broken pieces of Horus's missing eye.

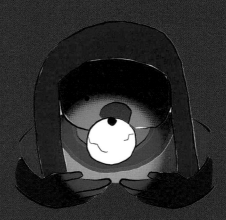

9. Thoth decided to put the missing eye together, and gives it back to Horus.

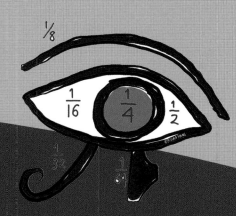

10. In such gratitude, Horus decides to give the eye to his father Osiris, which brings him back to life!

...The pieces of the Eye represented a specific fraction, just like in this illustration!

LET'S GET THINKING!

Write 2/3 as a sum of unit fractions.

Is there a part of Horus' eye still missing even after being reassembled?

Answers on Page 41!

14

ANCIENT GREEK MATHEMATICS

GREECE

Greece is famous for many things: art, architecture, science, philosophy and of course mathematics. Within Ancient Greek culture, providing persuasive argument was a highly regarded art form called "rhetoric". And in a society where being persuasive was fundamental, mathematics did not escape.

Instead of merely applying rules well tested by other civilisations, the Greeks wanted to be sure that what they knew empirically was always correct, no exceptions! This is how the mathematical proof emerged. And the first and very concrete example of that was the work of Euclid.

Euclid
325 BC–265BC

EUCLID AND THE ELEMENTS

Euclid's Elements is the oldest mathematical book that we know of (300BC). It is a mathematical treatise where Euclid set the foundations using some undeniable truths, and built more theorems and proofs around those. These irrefutable truths are called the "postulates", or "axioms" and there were five of them. We have to accept these as true in order to be able to use them as the basis of exploring more complex ideas. The five postulates were:

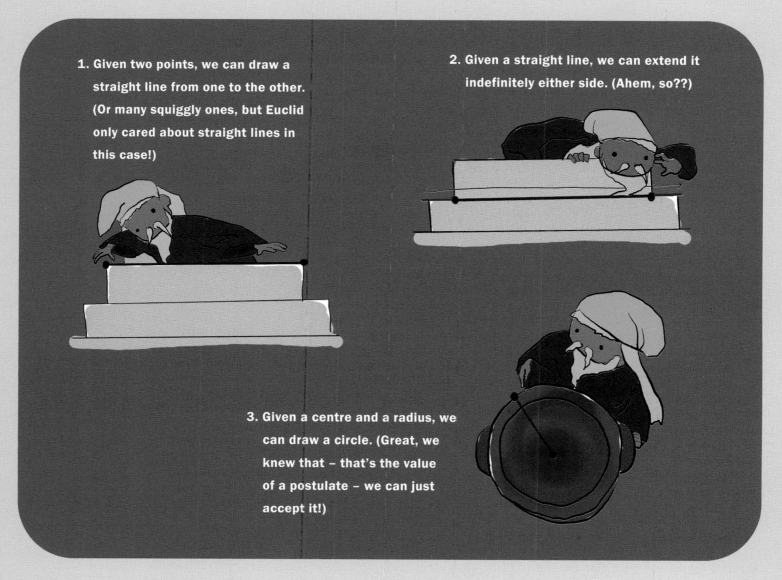

1. Given two points, we can draw a straight line from one to the other. (Or many squiggly ones, but Euclid only cared about straight lines in this case!)

2. Given a straight line, we can extend it indefinitely either side. (Ahem, so??)

3. Given a centre and a radius, we can draw a circle. (Great, we knew that – that's the value of a postulate – we can just accept it!)

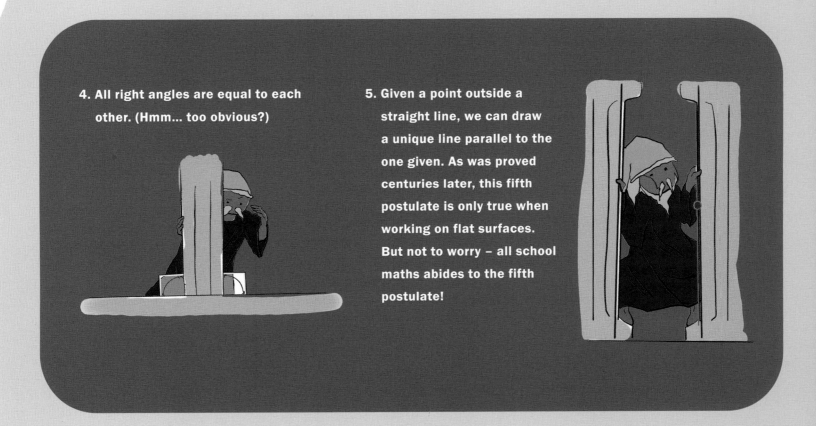

4. All right angles are equal to each other. (Hmm... too obvious?)

5. Given a point outside a straight line, we can draw a unique line parallel to the one given. As was proved centuries later, this fifth postulate is only true when working on flat surfaces. But not to worry – all school maths abides to the fifth postulate!

Euclid proved that the sum of angles in a triangle is the same as the sum of angles on a straight line, or 180 degrees.

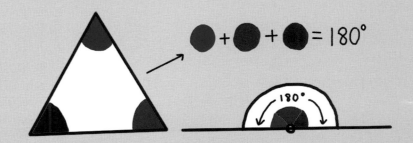

The diagram here is set up for the same purpose. How might you use this to prove that the sum of angles in a triangle is the same as the sum of angles on a straight line? Hint: Compare the angles formed around vertex A with the angles in the triangle.

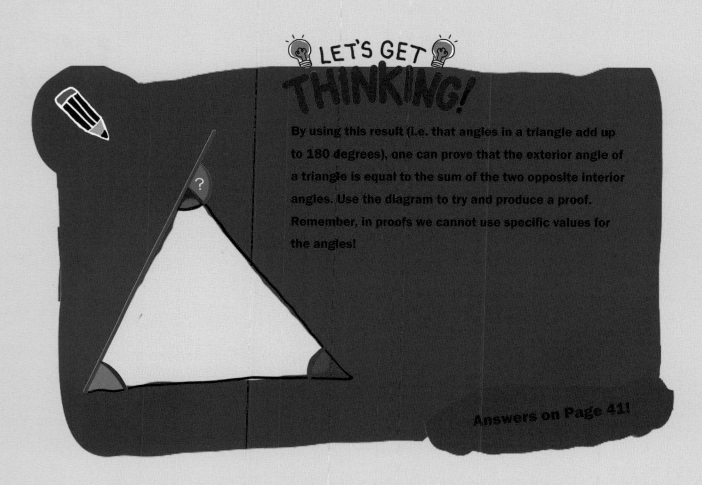

LET'S GET THINKING!

By using this result (i.e. that angles in a triangle add up to 180 degrees), one can prove that the exterior angle of a triangle is equal to the sum of the two opposite interior angles. Use the diagram to try and produce a proof. Remember, in proofs we cannot use specific values for the angles!

Answers on Page 41!

HELLENISTIC MATHEMATICS

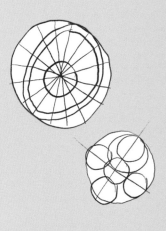

You may have noticed that not many female names have come up thus far (ok some of the names may have been unusual, but trust me, none of them were women). This continues to be true in the years following the Greeks. This is one of the reasons why Hypatia's story is so extraordinary! She taught at a university, at a time when women barely left their homes.

HYPATIA

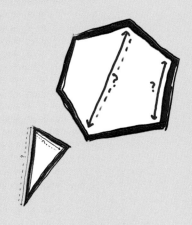

Hypatia worked on geometry, astronomy and number theory. She also taught philosophy at the University in Alexandria to large audiences of keen students. However, given the restrictions she faced as a woman, some of her work may have been an extension of that of others. Even more sadly, a deteriorating political situation in Alexandria resulted in her premature and brutal death. Despite this tragic end, her reputation and work have survived, and she is now enshrined as one of history's great women and an early symbol of feminism.

In this section dedicated to Hypatia we will look at some simplified number theory; that is the study of the relationships between positive integers (or whole numbers).

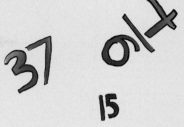

LET'S GET THINKING!

MULTIPLICATION	SQUARE NUMBER
EG: 1	1
2	4
3	9

Find two numbers x and y that have a difference of a and their squares have a difference of a+b, when a is 1 and b is 4. Challenge yourself even further by replacing a with 7 and b with 112!

Answers on Page 42!

$$9 = 3^2$$

Terminology reminders:
- *Difference* **is the result of subtraction**
- *Square* **is a number we obtain after we multiply any number by itself.**

E.g. in 3×3=9, the square number is 9.

Writing a list of the first 12 square numbers will help you solve this problem Hypatia may have set her students centuries ago!

HINDU-ARABIC MATHEMATICS

The Hindu-Arabic world not only translated and preserved ancient knowledge so that it survived Europe's dark ages, but it also gave us some very efficient ways to deal with problems. And it was in the Hindu-Arabic numbering system that zero finally acquired its place amongst all the other numbers.

AL-KHWARISMI

The words 'algorithm' and 'algebra' both owe their existence to the Persian mathematician and astronomer Al-Khwarismi. His contributions include advocating the Hindu-Arabic numbering system (our current numbering system), solving quadratic equations (equations where the unknown appears up to the power of two), and developing a generalised abstract language for solving problems. In fact, his name has become synonymous with the process of producing a fixed set of steps to solve problems of a certain type, after several transliterations, the algorithm!

The word algebra is found in the title of his book: 'Al-Kitab al-mukhtasar fi hisab **al-jabr** wa'l-muqabala', or "The Compendious Book on Calculation by Completion and Balancing" published in 830 AD. He described the method of simplifying expressions by removing terms from either side of an equation, and provided consistent methods for solving equations up to the second degree (that is equations where the unknown is squared).

> **Next up we'll see some examples of how we can simplify algebraic expressions, and try to crack the mystery!**

SIMPLIFYING EXPRESSIONS

Our notation is a bit newer than Al-Khwarismi's but he was the pioneer of rewriting expressions in simpler form.

How do we simplify $a+a+a$? Well, we don't go to the greengrocer's and ask for an apple and an apple and an apple, do we? We just ask for three apples. So, $a+a+a=3a$.

How about $a+2b+3a+b$? Again, you are very unlikely to ask for an apple and two bananas, and three apples and a banana. We just ask for four apples and three bananas. So, $a+2b+3a+b=4a+3b$.

What about expressions like $a+2b+ab$? Well, if you want an apple, two bananas and an apple-banana smoothie, there is no way to shorten that.

...Lastly, $a+a^2$ is about as complicated as it gets (including variations and combinations of the types so far mentioned of course), where a might be a length, and a^2 an area (buying ribbon and wrapping paper for example). So, again, the two cannot be merged.

LET'S GET THINKING!

Now try to simplify the expressions Below.

EXPRESSIONS TO SIMPLIFY	SIMPLIFIED VERSION	CHECKED ANSWER?
$a + 2a + b$		
$a + b + a + b$		
$a + b + ab + b$		
$a^2 + b + a + 3b$		
$a^3b + ab^2 + 2a^2b$		
$a + 3a + 2b - a$		
$a + ab + ab + a^2$		

Answers on Page 43!

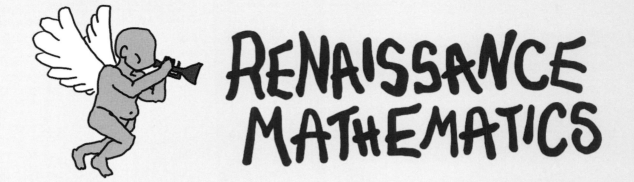

RENAISSANCE MATHEMATICS

After a long period of stagnation in Europe, the arts and sciences, mathematics included, began to flourish again in Italy around the 14th century. This period is known as the Renaissance.

FIBONACCI

Fibonacci was the first to introduce the new Hindu-Arabic numerals to Europe in his book Liber Abaci, or the book of calculation. It was also around this time that the symbols for plus and minus as we know them today start appearing in books.

Fibonacci's most famous problem was one about rabbit populations: if a pair of rabbits can reproduce one month after they are born, and continue to do so every month thereafter, how will the population of rabbits change over time?

$$\frac{1}{20} + \frac{1}{10} - 2 = x^2 - ab$$

$$+ - \div \times$$

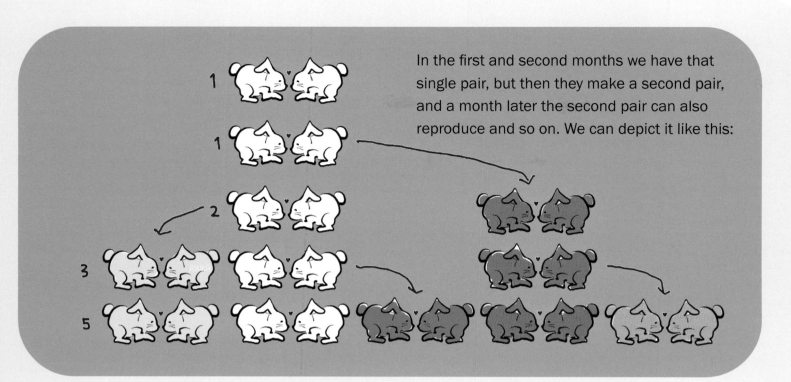

In the first and second months we have that single pair, but then they make a second pair, and a month later the second pair can also reproduce and so on. We can depict it like this:

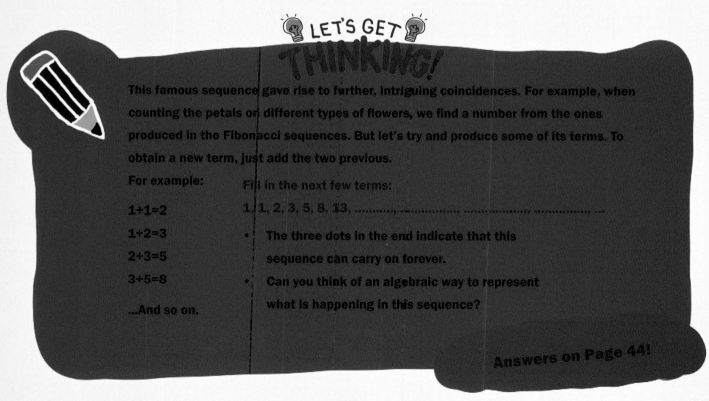

LET'S GET THINKING!

This famous sequence gave rise to further, intriguing coincidences. For example, when counting the petals on different types of flowers, we find a number from the ones produced in the Fibonacci sequences. But let's try and produce some of its terms. To obtain a new term, just add the two previous.

For example:

1+1=2

1+2=3

2+3=5

3+5=8

...And so on.

Fill in the next few terms:

1, 1, 2, 3, 5, 8, 13, ..., ..., ..., ..., ..., ...

• The three dots in the end indicate that this sequence can carry on forever.

• Can you think of an algebraic way to represent what is happening in this sequence?

Answers on Page 44!

EARLY MODERN MATHEMATICS

The Seven Bridges of Königsberg is a famous mathematical problem. In 1730s Prussia the citizens of Königsberg enjoyed the challenge of trying to get around their city without crossing the same bridge twice. The notorious difficulty of a seemingly simple task is probably what made it so famous. The map of the city looked a bit like this:

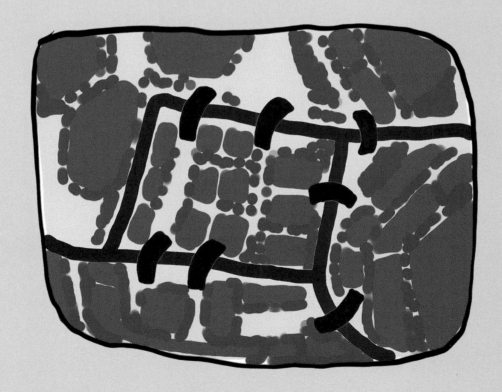

EULER

Euler was a Swiss mathematician who took an interest in this problem. What he noticed was that one did not actually need to go around the city to try and solve this problem, nor have multiple copies of the actual map. Instead, he thought of a way to simplify the map. Each of the four land regions – top bank, left island, right island and bottom bank – can be represented by a node (where the lines meet, represented by blue dots in the diagram). Each of the bridges can be represented by a line. The connections need to stay the same of course. So the map is now reduced to this diagram:

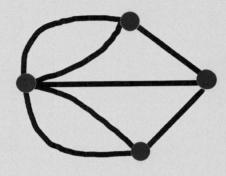

And the question becomes much simpler: can you trace this diagram without lifting your pencil (or going over the same line twice)? Go on, have a few goes at it!

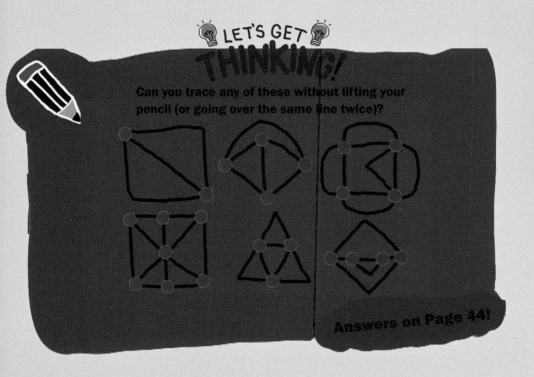

LET'S GET THINKING!

Can you trace any of these without lifting your pencil (or going over the same line twice)?

Answers on Page 44!

The easier ones to trace are those with an even number of lines connected to every node. You can start and end where you want! The ones with exactly two nodes with an odd number of lines are trickier. You have to start or end at one of the nodes that have the odd number of lines coming out of them. Finally, if you have more than two nodes with an odd number of lines, then the network you have created is untraceable.

...So what do you now think about the Seven Bridges of Konigsberg? Each of the four areas is connected with the others using an odd number of bridges. As all four nodes are odd, the problem was impossible to solve! That did not matter though, the mathematical ideas that were developed in trying to solve it, gave rise to some exciting new mathematics.

NETWORKS

Even for an untraceable network, one can still find efficient ways to go around. Network theory is used to help postmen and women deliver letters efficiently, or rubbish collectors follow the fastest route without unnecessarily using long roads more than once.

But network theory was not the only outcome from this unsolved problem! What Euler did by reducing his map to a simple diagram can be done for any map. For example, the map for the London underground is a simpler representation of a real map and allows us to understand routes and interchanges without confusing ourselves with extraneous surface detail.

LET'S GET THINKING!

Which features are kept and which are lost when creating an easy-to-use tube map?

Can you change these maps into a user-friendly simplified version using the principles Euler did?

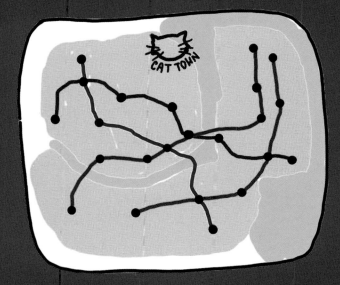

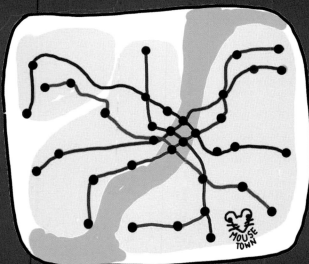

Answers on Page 45!

MODERN MATHEMATICS

Infinity, or endlessness, is a fascinating idea! We all come across it early on, when we learn to count, and we realise we could keep counting forever! (If we had nothing better to do...) This is the symbol for infinity.

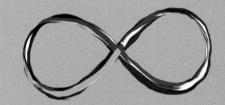

Because the symbol looks like an 8 on its side, the 8th day of the 8th month is known as Infinity Day. But most people are probably on holiday then, wishing it was infinite.

CANTOR AND INFINITE INFINITIES

Georg Cantor was a 19th-century German mathematician, who approached infinity in a novel way. He thought there might be different infinities, some bigger than others. This idea was not readily adopted, or even contested, and Cantor suffered for a long period. However, we now know he was right. There is an infinite number of different infinities. There are also sets of numbers that look different but in fact have the same infinity.

Consider the Natural numbers (the numbers we use to count): 1,2,3,4,5,6,7, ...
and the Even numbers (the positive multiples of two): 2,4,6,8,10,12,14,...
The three dots at the end denote that these sequences go on forever (so they are there for a reason).
Which set has more numbers, the Naturals or the Evens?

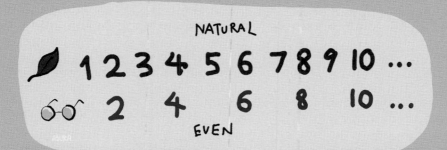

What a strange question I hear you think. Intuitively you probably want to say the Naturals since they contain all of the Evens, and more besides! But Cantor looked a bit more closely than that. Let's consider this thought experiment: If you choose a random Natural number, can you always find an Even to match it with? Yes! It's simple: just double the number you started with. In this way you get a one-to-one correspondence between the Naturals and the Evens and this shows they have the same infinity. It is called Countable Infinity, perhaps the strangest possible name for infinity. The symbol is aleph-zero:

ALEPH ZERO

Answers on Page 46!

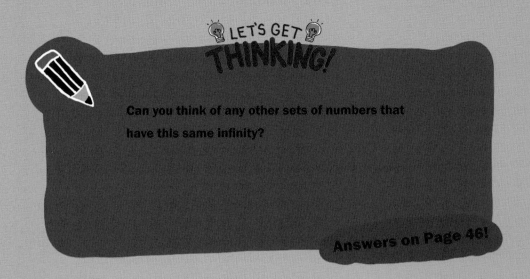

Can you think of any other sets of numbers that have this same infinity?

Any set of integer multiples will have the same infinity: multiples of 3, multiples of 4 and so on. But how about fractions? Our first suspicion could be that fractions are more than countably infinite. Besides, between zero and one we have half, between zero and half we have a quarter, between zero and a quarter we have an eight and so on.

And it is impossible to find a number that is immediately after half, or 0.5 (1/2). Would it be 0.51 (51/100)? How about 0.0501 (501/1000)? That's even closer! And how about 0.5000001 (5000001/10000000)? It's impossible to arrange these in order of size. But Cantor came up with this amazing idea of listing fractions without considering their size but rather their position.
See the image on the next page!

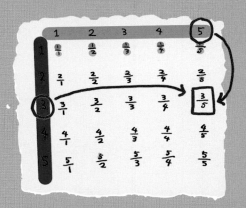

This diagram is built by using all the fractions with numerator equal to one in the first row, numerator equal to two in the second row and so on. Similarly, any fraction with denominator one is found in the first column, denominator two in the second column etc.

So we can find 3/5 by looking at the third row and fifth column. We can list these fractions in one to one correspondence with the Natural Numbers, so, again, the fractions have countable infinity too. And this is only the beginning!

The next set of numbers worth looking into would be the set of real numbers. These numbers can all be written as decimals may or may not follow a pattern. Let's try to create a list with all of them, in random order:

0.2849602...
1.9494500...
0.4861123...
0.5568483...

.... And so on.

Let's now create a decimal number by taking the first digit from the first number on our list, second digit from the second number and so on. Each time we will be adding one to that digit, and if it is a nine we will turn it into a zero. So we will get this number:

1.097...

Let's now check if this number we just created is in our original list. It cannot be the first number as they differ in the first digit; it cannot be the second as they differ in the second digit and so on. This means that the number we created is not in the list, so we cannot produce a list of all Real numbers;

Real numbers have a bigger infinity than the natural numbers. That's just the first set that we know of with a bigger infinity, but there are infinite more sets with even bigger infinities. But that is something you might want to study later on!

Your Mathematical Adventures journey has now come to an end. Be sure to revisit the stories that you found most fascinating or when more inexplicable things come up! And remember, the events in this book hardly say the whole story. So well done for being adventurous and do continue to explore the fascinating world of mathematics.

So much more is left to be discovered. And who knows, maybe you'll also discover something someday and then a section about you might be added!

The answers to the activities are in the following pages. Have you got them all correctly?

The Lebombo Bone Activity

1. Jan (31), Feb (28/29 for a leap year), Mar (31), Apr (30), May (31), Jun (30), Jul (31), Aug (31), Sep (30), Oct (31), Nov (30), Dec (31).

You can easily find this using the knuckles and the dips between them on your hand and saying the months in order. If you land on a knuckle, the month has 31 days, if you land in a dip, the month has 30 (unless it's February when it has even fewer). Our calendar has not always been as it is today and in early calendars February used to be the last month so this could be the reason why it has fewer days than the rest (i.e. the ones left over!).

2. It took a long time before the additional day ever four years was introduced. To account for the ".25" in the duration of a year, one could play around with the number of days in each month (rumour has it that Augustus Caesar added a day in August which had his name). I suppose it would be nice if we could add some more days to the summer months.

3. Dimensions (24cm x 24cm)

Round to the next whole number for wrapping paper and even to the next ten for a gift bag. Be careful not to round to the nearest whole number or ten, as rounding to something slightly smaller than the actual dimensions of the book could mean that it does not fit. For posting all you need to do is consider whether its width would allow it to go through the mail slot on your front door; if not, it is a parcel, not a letter and the pricing is different.

GRAB A PEN!

The Ishango Bone Activity

a.   **2 (1 or 2)**
b.   **2 (1 or 3)**
c.   **3 (1 or 2 or 4)**
d.   **2 (1 or 5)**
e.   **4 (1 or 2 or 3 or 6)**

f.   **2 (1 or 7)**
g.   **4 (1 or 2 or 4 or 8)**
h.   **3 (1 or 3 or 9)**
i.   **4 (1 or 2 or 5 or 10)**

The ones that only work for 2 groups of people are **prime numbers**. The groups they work for are their **factors**.

The Numbering Systems activity

The Factors of **60** are:
1, 2, 3, 4, 5, 6, 10, 12, 15, 20, 30, 60

MODERN	BABYLONIAN	MAYAN
12	⟨ＹＹ	2 (20) + 10
55		2 (20) + 10 + 5
111		100 + 11 (10 + 1)
360	(60 + 51)	300 + 3 (20) 0
	6 (60)	

The Rhind Mathematical Papyrus activity

Houses:	7 (7^1)		**Grains of barley:**	2401 (7^4)
Cats:	49 (7^2)		**Hekats of barley:**	16807 (7^5)
Mice:	343 (7^3)		**Total:**	19607 ($7^1+7^2+7^3+7^4+7^5$)

The Eye of Horus Activity

Unit Fractions:

$$\frac{2}{3} = \frac{1}{2} + \frac{1}{6}$$

Part of the Eye left:

$$1 - \left(\frac{1}{2} + \frac{1}{4} + \frac{1}{8} + \frac{1}{16} + \frac{1}{32} + \frac{1}{64} \right) = \frac{1}{64}$$

Euclid and The Elements

PROOF 1

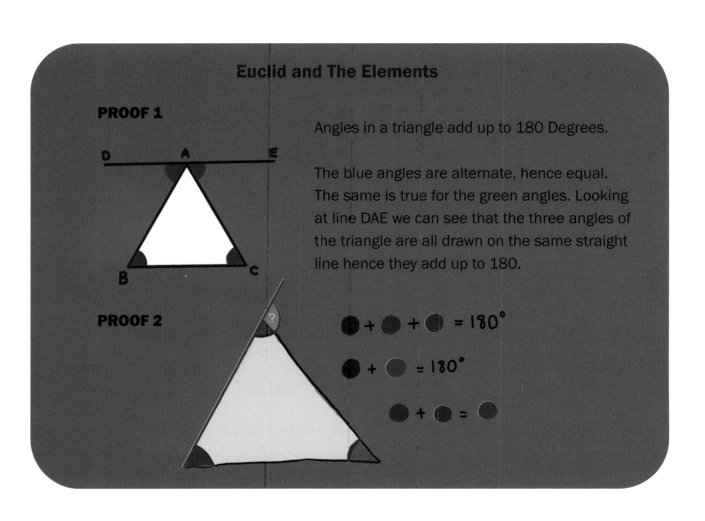

Angles in a triangle add up to 180 Degrees.

The blue angles are alternate, hence equal. The same is true for the green angles. Looking at line DAE we can see that the three angles of the triangle are all drawn on the same straight line hence they add up to 180.

PROOF 2

● + ● + ● = 180°

● + ● = 180°

● + ● = ●

Hypatia Activity

MULTIPLICATION	SQUARE NUMBER
1×1	1
2×2	4
3×3	9
4×4	16
5×5	25
6×6	36
7×7	49
8×8	64
9×9	81
10×10	100
11×11	121
12×12	144

Solution for a = 1 and b = 4:

x = 4 and **y = 3**.

Solution for a = 7 and b = 112:

x = 12 and **y = 5**

Al-Khwarismi Activity

EXPRESSIONS TO SIMPLIFY	SIMPLIFIED VERSION
$a + 2a + b$	$3a + b$
$a + b + a + b$	$2a + 2b$
$a + b + ab + b$	$a + 2b + ab$
$a^2 + b + a + 3b$	$a^2 + a + 4b$
$a^2b + ab^2 + 2a^2b$	$3a^2b + ab^2$
$a + 3a + 2b - a$	$3a + 2b$
$a + ab + ab + a^2$	$a + a^2 + 2ab$

Fibonacci Activity

1, 1, 2, 3, 5, 8, 13, 21, 34, 55, 89, ...

To describe this sequence using algebraic terms we need to use indicators, small writing lower than the rest, to show us the order in the sequence:

$$a_n = a_{n-1} + a_{n-2}$$

The subscript tells us that we need to move two positions back and then one position back and add what we find in those positions to arrive at the term in the current (nth) position. This is known as a recursive formula because it makes use of previous findings.

Euler Tracing Activity

The two Tracable Shapes have no more than two odd numbers of lines coming out of the nodes, and / or are all even numbered!

GO!

Activity on The Seven Bridges (Tube Map)

Kept: sequence of stations, different tube lines (and, say, their chosen colours), connections between stations.

Lost: shape of lines, measurements (distances are not proportional: by looking at the tube map you cannot be sure which stations are further apart or closer together)

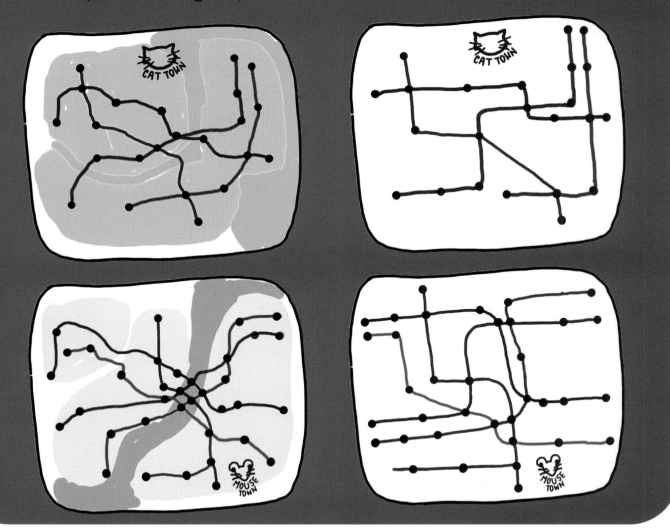